FLYWAY

also by Sarah Ens

The World Is Mostly Sky

FLYWAY

Sarah Ens

TURNSTONE PRESS

Flyway
copyright © Sarah Ens 2022
Turnstone Press
Artspace Building
206-100 Arthur Street
Winnipeg, MB
R3B 1H3 Canada
www.TurnstonePress.com

All rights reserved. No part of this book may be reproduced or transmitted in any form or by any means—graphic, electronic or mechanical—without the prior written permission of the publisher. Any request to photocopy any part of this book shall be directed in writing to Access Copyright, Toronto.

Turnstone Press gratefully acknowledges the assistance of the Canada Council for the Arts, the Manitoba Arts Council, the Government of Canada through the Canada Book Fund, and the Province of Manitoba through the Book Publishing Tax Credit and the Book Publisher Marketing Assistance Program.

Cover design: Jonathan Dyck
Cover image: ribbed plant-leap print by Meghan Harder

Printed and bound in Canada.

Library and Archives Canada Cataloguing in Publication

Title: Flyway / Sarah Ens.
Names: Ens, Sarah, 1992- author.
Description: Poems.
Identifiers: Canadiana (print) 20220168393 | Canadiana (ebook) 20220168423 | ISBN 9780888017567 (softcover) | ISBN 9780888017574 (EPUB) | ISBN 9780888017581 (PDF)
Classification: LCC PS8609.N72 F59 2022 | DDC C811/.6—dc23

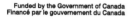

for my grandmothers

FLYWAY

a long poem

Prelude

There is this place, this patch of tallgrass, a grassland of bluestem, wheatgrass, prairie cordgrass tall to my shoulders. Hardy bunchgrass, swaying. I'd never thought much about grass until I came to this place, but here the thought of grass is inescapable, everywhere innumerous "thrones, / dominions of grass" bending. Six thousand square kilometres of tallgrass once ran along the Red River Valley (imagine). Less than one percent remains. What remains: this small place, this preserve, here. It survives along a flyway—a flight path between breeding & wintering grounds spanning continents & oceans, stringing together places like this. So, the birds, too, I notice here: warblers, swallows, meadowlarks, migratory birds who rely on this place. My gaze tumbles from sky to shrub, poorly tracking flutters & specks & song.

Not knowing, I hunch under clouds, blustery light falling into the grass. I am here to think about grass & birds. To ask & look & listen. I am here a descendent of Mennonite settlers in the land of the Anishinaabeg, Assiniboine, Dakota, & Cree, the homeland of the Métis. Mennonites a people displaced (displacing), so goes the story carried from Switzerland, South Germany, Netherlands, Austria, Hungary, Poland, Prussia, Ukraine. Some stories follow you your whole life & spill out in front of you, flight paths well worn. Here we stayed, the Mennonites, converting tallgrass to farmland & claiming it as home.

Many voices burble under rising threat, overwhelming peril. They hum in the grass. & here I am, listening. & here I am with this story.

Tallgrass Psalmody

PART ONE

What brings you to nest?

Not wings, though
the body's branches
quiver. Some squall,
some sense
of service or
sentry stirred you
from city, so
lift your head,
look.

   & what do you bring to the nest?

   All knotted sorrow!
   How sorry you are,
   wishing to make peace
   in this breeding
   place, make
   stone & sedge
   from struggle. Do
   you know struggle?
   Watch here how
   earth spreads out
   like sea, cold wet-
   land heaving.
   This ground
   bends sudden under
   sky. Follow suit.

                      I will try to tell the truth
                      to the blood feather tangled in the reeds.

                I don't know what I thought would happen
                          when I came to this last stand
                                  of tallgrass
               holding field guides, family archives, & prayer
                        stones in my hands.

                    Am I close? Am I warm? I am sitting here
                                      in dirt.

Have you heard the flight songs?

Sandpipers shape-shift, spill
from sky. They shimmer
swarm, wade
in the wind, trill
names for home.
Ask about
the huge, the
hollow, the wild
open mouth of land,
now here,
now hungry,
now
hush.

                                                The broken feather means
                                                          something,
                                                   I think, squint
                                                  its serrated edge.

Will you get on your knees?

Your shame, lodged
like a stone, sinks you,
so suck up breath
& laugh—
for a lark, try to feel
how rain sweeps over
earth in waves.
Swiftly now,
falter to basin,
slip, slide
thunder-spooked,
creep to belly broad
with bog. Swat
air bug-thick, cover
your eyes, your
ears. They'll find
dusk's ripe blood,
tick & fly, they'll eat
you through.

Wonder what swoops
in shadow, what feasts:
flycatchers, swallows,
grassland & boreal birds
beak-full. They scoop the
droning horde, clean
out the air—
polychlorinated
biphenyls,
polycyclic aromatic
hydrocarbons,
neonicotinoids,
poisoned arrows
meet their marks. Scratch,
shuck your skin
where it swells.

                                         Out-flung under sky,
                      I read letters, diaries, strange & plaintive
                                              poems.

I don't know what I'm listening for.

bank swallow; barn swallow; eastern whip-poor-will; common nighthawk; common yellowthroat; least flycatcher; eastern wood-pewee; whip-poor-will; whip-poor-will

Will you stand in the switchgrass exalting?

Come frailty,
come fledgling—
O think well
of your meeting &
cast all lines for
flyway! Plunge
feet deep to the mud,
drum down, moult
open-mouthed
in preparation for
sky-wide homing.
If sluggish
your heart, know
blood as branching,
tuggish, un-shushed.
Shriek, yes, wail all
your loss asunder,
but see: each crest
of quill, each
plummet, stroke,
swish, & claw
as a returning
to roost. Come
magnetic, come urging,
orient in
migrant's memory.

Under my nylon hood, I read:
*unrelenting headwinds can change
whole flocks to stones
    dropping from sky.*

I read: *what we did to survive.*

I stand in the switchgrass
  & read the wind the way I want it.

Have you sheltered from storm?

Or have you blown
so far off course?
Find bearings in
daylight hot
& caught in
shoots blue, green,
blue waking gold.
Sundrop, cynthia,
deep needlegrass,
dropseed, feel these
roots eking long thread
maps, lightning-forked
but tender, converting
the dark.

        Shivering in pale sun,
          I imagine warblers
        huddled in shaking grass,
         their tiny bodies still
          between my feet.

How do you unfold bones for flight?

Not honestly—some
malice uplifts you.
For now, hold
still & till all under.
They won't last,
your puny roots.
Learn to put your
self in the
ending: lie
in the vanishing,
the bright eyes,
the sky lurch.

                Swallows spiral against wind which wails into sky.

& how do you sleep?

Not easy, it's
clear, your conscience
shakes up since
this became no
home to return
to. So brood awake,
shape a nest the
full length
of your longing,
& tell
in this dry
place some
small story.

Flight

1929-1945

Anni

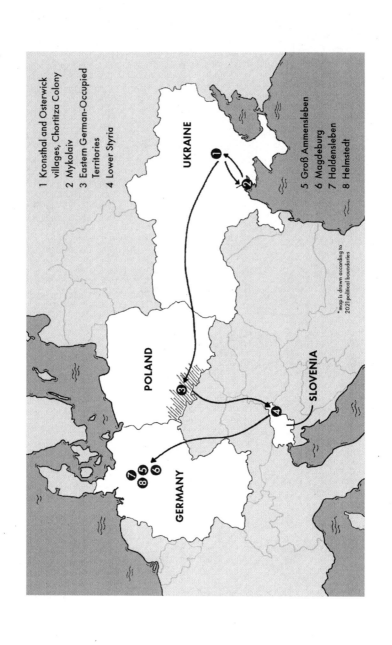

Kronsthal, Soviet Ukraine

The first Lydia came loud and red, fists and feet. Mother hurt
my wrist squeezing, her skirt hitched to hips, until the midwife

caught the slipping baby, pronounced her girl, sister, everything
I'd been hoping. Then Lydia's body filled with lead.

The eldest at six, my job became strapping her to a narrow
wooden board, careful to mind her lolling. I practised Russian

or sang her the old songs while Hans, only four, grubbed
her hair, her bright, wet mouth. He cried when she moaned

so I kept her from him, never left her on the floor,
felt her eyes sweep the flush of my face.

The first Lydia lived two years and died before the killing
hunger. That year, Peter came, our little boy in blue.

Spring. Everything mud. The minister helped Mother move
Lydia board to box. Father upright in the grave.

The minister prayed in our language and my shoulders ached
with the memory of her weight and I do not remember release,

only that the second Lydia rolled, sat up, held my fingers.
When I rocked her, I cooed *Lida*, and that year

our churches closed.
Mother often cried behind the house.

Hunger taught us to wake slowly, to lift, as if from water.
If you did not starve, hunger taught you

to watch and wait. If you did not starve,
the stone of your stomach turned traitor. Father was waiting,

but I do not know who pointed the police at him. I know
Mother screamed, once. I thought I saw them shoot him
            in the head. I didn't hear anything.

I saw my father on his knees.
Father's anger, a storm I knew, kneeling.

He took with him the Bible from the kitchen table and Mother
ran to the neighbours to borrow money, told me *Anni, stay*

so from the door I watched my father walk the road
to the Black Raven full of men. He did not look up at the night.

Mother pressed her face into his hands.

Lida, from her cradle, howling.   In the kitchen,
Mother stood, bent over the stove,

and shook. I got sick and the village emptied of men.
The Black Raven ate them all.

Mother tried, once, to learn where they'd taken Father,
travelled to a holding jail in Zaporizhzhia with some clothes,

a woollen coat. They took his things, told her nothing.
After that, assigned to work in the stables,

placed in charge of calves, she began slipping
ground oats and wheat, bottles of milk

to the pockets of her dress,
hummed hymns arranging the table at home.

And the calves in her care—
Mother won a prize for the district's best herd.

Shaping wells in flour
for milk, oil, eggs, salt,

I'd show Lida, perched,
how to pinch fruit and curds to each

square's centre, *take up two corners
to make a triangle*, while

Peter read me my textbooks,
wrote in my answers, hurried calculations

between boiled cabbage and potatoes,
cream and klops, kielke with sausage,

the washing, mending, tending,
pickles, preserves, potatoes, potatoes,

Peter throwing rocks from the field and singing.
He'd wring his fingers of dirt

and I'd rub them warm, heat milk until scalded,
make a rough dough come alive with the heels of my hands.

Hans brought the water and wood looking hungry,
hungry almost like Father, tall but hunching,

shaking dust from his hair. He prayed over dinner,
forgive us our trespasses, slow and shy and nothing

like Father. Mother's heavy steps back from the stables.
Night spilling in, we'd scrub the floor.

Take two corners, fold a triangle.
Press open edges firmly.

Lida, a little bird.
When she couldn't sleep,

we'd imagine dough
pulled to smooth

springing satin. In dreams,
the house all corners

and squeezed tight
as a fist.

Osterwick, Soviet Ukraine

A blur of hands and skirts and curls. Did I laugh?
It spun from me like smoke, hot and full. If I laughed,

I ached with it. Look, these Soviet boys jumping,
legs wide, stomping to ground, quick as drums.

Could you hear it to the moon, their far-flung feet?
And me, soon off to Simferopol, my scholarship

spinning me somewhere new, into something
immense, endless—I could reach

up, catch my dress, stamp the world solid,
turn and turn and turn.

We must have laughed; we trembled with it.
The storm we knew, kneeling.

The party broke at six in the morning. We were so proud,
you could hear it to the moon. In the buggy that took me home,

I held my cheeks, puffed to my palms, pulled in all the air
I could, this blur of leaping and leaping and loud in the landing.

I almost laughed, the next day. To have danced,
to have ever danced,

when the next day, the Germans invaded.

Soviet village

That summer, we dug for Stalin, dug ourselves
to the ground somewhere west of the village,

Hitler's men almost at the Dnieper. Bodies squatting, standing,
shovelling clay, metal on stone, the noise and stink

and all of us digging. Most of us kept our heads down,
turning scorched earth, but Mother looked around,

said *Well, someone has to feed them.* She prayed the Germans
would collect us; until then, I'd play cook, sweat steam,

peel translucent leaves of cabbage, holloptsee slopped
to bowls held in soldiers' outstretched hands.

I saw, when I slept   tanks rolling over our fields.

Kronsthal, Soviet Ukraine

Early August, the Soviets let us return
long enough for Mother to make bread,

pull dishes from the cupboard,
trace their chips, put them back.

Lida and Peter rejoiced in what remained:
the sun all afternoon stretching down the hall,

here, the old stain on the tablecloth,
here, the garden where the first Lydia sleeps.

Then: *The front is coming. Pack.*

Island of Chortitza, Soviet Ukraine

Trembling in dirt, everyone looks animal.
Listen for the river on fire, sky howling flame, primal prayer.

I might have opened my mouth too, but when someone
started crying, Mother's fingers dug the soft skin of my wrist.

Keep quiet, Anni, keep your whole self a firm line.
Out over the Dnieper, the Germans held the bridge.

Airplanes growled, riverbank ablaze. Under bunkers,
low in fallow fields, families from the village hid.

I kept count of those I could see, Peter flinching against me.
I tucked his hair under his hat. We'd shuttled the first bridge.
        Now there was nowhere

to run, river split around us. Body to body,
I held my breath to stop the smell.

The Soviets had told us to take only what we could carry,
told us to take what we could, but the men

to go on ahead—the men and all movable assets.
Hans in the doorway, hat in hands.

I said *Be safe, Brother, come back* and he grinned, briefly,
stooped to let Mother touch his cheek   hold
his sharp shoulders.

Working the cattle beside the wagons,
he joined a slow caravan smeared into the road

then gone entirely.

I might have opened my mouth then,
or in the shelter by the bridge,

but Lida cried even sleeping
and Peter said *Shh*, stretched to hold her hand.

Beneath the Oak of Chortitza

Outside the bunker, an oak, and some girls gathered
under its canopy, old arms twisting

cathedral. Head rolled back against bark,
a Ukrainian girl said her people

had come to these roots for generations
and generations, worshipped here, sought sanctuary.

Almost all men and half the women and children
gone from the villages east of the Dnieper.

My cousin hugged her knees to her chin,
found an acorn folded in the fabric of her dress.

I held her wrist, cool, a pulse, a proverb,
bullets in bursts from the bridge.

Tree trembling. Terror
                      a long river cringing through the earth.

Kronsthal, Occupied Ukraine

Crawling from the bomb shelter,
we cheered.

The bridge was blown,
and the dam,

but our salvation
had survived the night.

The Germans allowed us to go home,
though the road was full

with mangled wagons, things
that used to matter to people,

and people,
dead on the road.

In the village, everything broken
or gone.

In the village, our mayor
gave thanks.

> *We are free! The brave German troops*
> *rescued us from the damn Bolshevistic yoke!*

In the village, we stood together, cried,
and set to work.

Mykolaiv, Occupied Ukraine

An ethnic German with her Russian education
was a natural ally of the Reich. I could work

my Soviet-split tongue. I could hear the Black Sea
wailing, weighted, full of bodies, my dreams all bloat and bog.

Awake, I translated furniture factory orders across borders, untangled
    customers' codes, complaints, sent money home,

Mother's letter laughing in my ear: *To think—*
Germans and Russians swapping loveseats!

Nazis through Zaporizhzhia advancing. Now and again
hushed word about our Jewish neighbours—

in dreams I saw deep water swelling.

Thought I misread the news of Hans's return. Too miraculous;
I believed Mother sick with seeing ghosts.

Still, I took the next train, sank to sleep
against the window's fogged glass,

the Sea rushing   speaking somewhere in the dark.

Kronsthal, Occupied Ukraine

Hans insisted he walk me to the library,
soldiers stationed at every other corner. Another downpour.

The road sucked on our boots. I tried to run
while beside me Hans stepped in slow motion.

He wouldn't say how he'd snuck away and returned to us;
I didn't ask. We ducked into the library together. Before,

our village boasted almost three hundred Bolshevik books,
but they'd all been destroyed. I stood dripping in the dust

while Hans scraped mud from his soles. German newspapers
a neat stack on a shelf. There was nothing else.

I tucked a paper under my coat,
Hans held another over us,
        and we stepped back into the rain.

Mykolaiv, Occupied Ukraine

Bent over my kitchen table, we rolled dough for perishky
with plums. Lida had spent the day picking flowers to press

in her book for luck, clusters from a guelder rose
blooming in her pocket. Still giddy from the train ride alone,

her first visit to the city, she drew shapes in the flour, giggled
that Hans had a girlfriend, why else would he disappear so often,

and at night; Mother folding his shirts, making his bed,
saying nothing when he came home with the sun.

Flour formed a fuzzed line along the bridge of Lida's nose,
plum juice ran down my palm.

I sucked on a pit and remembered:

Oma's orchard in the summer,
shade and the smell of apples, pears, plums.
All the adults up in Oma's big house making roast,
a celebration after threshing, and me in the orchard on my belly,
        pushing plum pits into the earth.

Lida said Oma and our aunts were well, Peter and Hans too,
really, and Mother always worried, but things had mostly gone

back to how they were.

Kronsthal, Occupied Ukraine

I do not know premonition.

I did not see it, when Peter drowned.

But I knew hope, how it punished.

His teacher said he swam too far.

An accident, we were told,

in the midst of war.

I came home for the burial, but I was not well.

I tried to swallow stones.

I could not eat anything but earth.

I put it in my mouth.

Mother pulled me from the road.

His skinny arms my mother said.

Where is God my mother said.

I saw his body blue beneath a smooth skin of water.

I saw his body blue.

How I shook pale light from wet grass, stumbled
a snow-smell up from dirt, how Peter's rubber boots

stood off the road like he had just stepped out,
then his sweater, blue wool a bright scraggy flag

in the field, how I followed the boy's breadcrumbs
to the barn, how, from the hayloft, his yellow hair

stuck full of straw, he said *I cannot come down!
These swallows believe I am wanting their nests!*

and how the birds streamed through the door, how
Peter's knees, round with fat, crouched

above that morning's dust, *Will you catch me, Anni?*
flinging himself, a slight shadow swooped

along the barn wall, how
his two bare feet collided with my chest

then swung round my hips,
how we clung to each other

under the swallows' rapid swarm,
and how
                                      how

        it looked like

                    he was sleeping
how Hans   hid his crying how

Lida curled around herself   and our mother
straight-backed
              how her hands

lay empty in her lap.

Mykolaiv, Occupied Ukraine

Lida's letter read:

Anni, church is open!
I wore your brown beret and Mama says the new minister
is too young. Hans sits on the men's side with the rest of the boys,
all treble. We had faspa after service and someone brought portzeltje.
It didn't matter it's past New Year's. Hans ate six at least!

My letter read:

Mama, what do you know of Stalingrad?
They say two million dead or imprisoned.
Civilians crushed in trenches.

Mama, what do you know of German defeat?
Stalin will come to claim us.
He is not stopped.

River, Occupied Ukraine

We waited by water's dark shroud praying safe crossing.
Those two weeks in grey October, Mother huddled
      with our aunts and Oma far up the bank

while Lida stabbed sticks into sand, dredged trenches,
said she was building forts. Hans smoked, cupping bright flame

with long fingers.   He wanted to help the Nazis rebuild

the bombed-out bridge, but Mother kept him close,
the Red Army arriving any moment, Mother's head in her hands.

For two weeks I knelt by the river and piled stones,
a grave to mark each moving body.

I knew evacuees crawled the road behind us,
35,000 stumbling through the murk. You could hear

their hungry animals in the night, the digging of shallow pits
to hold their dead.

I watched ice creep bright over the surface of the water.
Jesus walked like that, soft steps through a storm,
      a refugee in day's plain view.

Somewhere along the German/Polish border

In the mirror, red lipstick, curled hair   someone
who could laugh, be asked to dance.

Lida pranced, her first party, my dress hemmed for her, taken in,
and Mother's earrings lined across her palm.

She chose plastic pearls, snapped one to each lobe, shuddered
with delight. In the mirror, I watched myself:

a lifted brow, blush rubbed across cheeks, a white neck,
thin blue veins. Two dark brown eyes.

Blink. A chest filling, falling. A night out there

with music, men.   Soldiers' hands and sour breath.
The girl in the mirror, staring.

O du fröhliche, O du selige, O how hard
the snow fell from black sky.

We stood close to make a big singing sound,
all of us who'd lost our men.

The old ones weeping for that winter, the whole world
lost, but for Christ   born at the border   born

of Soviet soldiers, Nazi soldiers, soldiers
   seizing in the night,

but the makeshift church, the candle glow, the sure soprano
sending stars to follow, rejoice,
       rejoice,

O Christenheit, our small circle,
what we did to survive.

At least we were together, aunts and cousins,
Oma, Hans and Lida, our mother, all learning to pick up and go
       and go again.

Those loud nights I dreamed of barn swallows
come from Africa, their fluttered bodies spun to one long wing,

darting calls warbling over ocean. I would wake shaking,
little birds lost to storms.

Hans barely slept, smoked all night, grew smaller,
 and when they sent us on again in trucks,
        they kept him,

every Kronsthaler boy who could march, hold a German gun.

        Mother wept *You turned back before* but we knew

he could not twice. Hans stood shifting, crossed
one leg behind the other while Mother

warbled.   *Please God.*
Hans would not let her kiss him goodbye. I dreamed
        birds fell from the sky.

Mountainside, Lower Styria, Occupied Yugoslavia

Dirty rags. A gold-painted
picture frame. Glass
        smashed. A spoon. Someone's

doll, her hair in braids.
Song book   recipes,
encyclopedia

        of birds. And us, told
to settle, Lida too old

to hold Mother's
skirt like this   with such

hard fists.
Our Oma, aunts, cousins
sent to some

        different hill
in the distant range—there

        out the window
left open. And what
were we to do?   We were

who we were.
We stood   together, cried,

and then we set to work.

Hans's letter read:

Dear Mama, we arrived on Tuesday.
Spent the night walking around the city and not finding
what we were looking for. The clothes from home I no longer need.
I do not know what to do with the clothes.
We are fed but the food does not taste good.
We have to march and are learning to shoot. Dear Mama,
I have to do as ordered. I cannot turn back.
Mama, I am not doing very well. Please send me some food.
If only I could go home again.
My dear Mama, why can I not do that?

Mother said:

You must visit him, Anni.
Bring with you food and cigarettes.
Tell him how we pray.

Maribor, Lower Styria, Occupied Yugoslavia

A grey hill and the wind almost knocking me over.
Hans in the wind. Dark wool draped too loose   swastika spun

round his arm. I could not imagine him marching
but saw clearly his capture, thin fingers spread to sky, defeat

already in the grey of his face. *They're sending us to Poland*
        the crumbling Eastern Front.

Under me, hill grew to mountain, so I dropped to my knees.
As prisoner, he would go to Siberia and Siberia would break him.

I could see him:

after Father's arrest, Hans just twelve and in the field,
a skinny boy hunched up beside what men were left.

He only learned to read because I made him.
He'd roll his knuckles on the table, clench his teeth,

swear himself red and almost choking, would rather
clean machines   plough earth to straight rows.

Then, not in the field, but in the barn, I saw him:

on a milking stool where the women sat, the slouch of his spine
a sharp line of stones. The flank of a cow, her heavy sway,

and Hans with his face against the broad warmth,
his eyes closed, no,
             weeping.

From the grey hill he would go to Poland then Siberia,
my brother, now nineteen and twisting his hands in front of him.

Anni he said. He said my name until I looked at him.

How do you remember home?

Mountainside, Lower Styria, Occupied Yugoslavia

Fine thread through her fingers, spiralled
round her thumb. To web a rainbow, Lida lifted her hand,

                        let late morning light through.
A winter outside shredded by the mountain's teeth,
but inside, bright summer marigold plucked from the spool.

Zheltyy Lida said like I taught her,
Russian surprising, funny to her once   now slow, low,

zhovtyy she tried, then *gelb, jäl*, unwinding colour,
swirling it to the floor, sighing my latest lesson: *yellow,*
    oh-yellow-oh, oh, oh.

The purges taught us to sleep light, spill our eyes
into a shifting dark. I felt Mother stir, reach for my wrist,

breath light on my cheek.

        The Partisani are coming.

We ran the mountain awake, Mother gasping *Unlatch the door.*
Our aunts' faces pale under black kerchiefs,

us pleading they come, pulling their hands, then praying,
Mother and her sisters bowed low around the table.

They said they could not leave: David, their boy,
taken months ago, *What if he returns and finds this home empty?*

I saw Hans on the hill   blinked, bowed
into the bedroom where Oma sat up, smiled
when she saw me.

        That first winter in Siberia—
Oma would survive only three weeks. Our aunts almost starve.
They'd eat potatoes frozen in the ground and in spring,
roots, weeds, the first green things that came from the earth.

Mother and Lida and I—
              we turned our backs and ran.

Groß Ammensleben, Germany

Kneeling in the little church, I waited for the ground to shake,
but the floorboards held firm.

    Yes, I do believe.

The minister read to me in German. *A Lutheran!* Mother said,
but his instruction carried me to this baptismal font.

    Yes   I do believe,

all these makeshift cabins together, us who fled
the Partisani   and the Front   and the Red Army

on and on and through the mountains.
The Lutheran sprinkled water across my forehead,

water cold from the river. I saw it splashing up into a boat
    and the boat not sinking   water
calling us home.

    Yes, I do believe,

all of us who fled to the barracks
where I cooked and fed because I could,

I knew how, and knew, too,
how to survive   the soldiers   how to stay
    very still

    with the help of God.

I felt the Lutheran's fingers
        draw a cross above my closed eyes.

Peter in the river.
All deep water taking us home,

and a candle lighting Lida's face.

Her closed eyes.
Sure that I could only crawl,

        Yes, with the help of God,

I stood.

Magdeburg, Germany

For a time, I travelled every day to work at an architect's office,
stare at drawings of buildings skeletal,

imagined. One morning when I arrived, the city in flames.
                        I covered my face.

Smoke, taste of ash   burning dead. I could not see—
bombed by Allied planes, the whole city   gone.

Behind me, passengers tumbled from the train.
A woman grabbed my arm. *We could have been here*

when it happened—her eyes red seams across her face.

Haldensleben, Germany

The war ended but the world unended. Mother said
  Keep your eyes and ears open and everywhere.

Behind my rented room's thin walls, I waited, hushed,
       found work as an occupation interpreter.

German surrender   Soviet rule   and men's
                                            muffled voices.

Then February, and Churchill and Roosevelt allowed Stalin
  to send   liberated Soviet citizens   home.

      Mennonites I heard through the office door
repatriated   no home
to return to.

That night I counted my breaths   packed   caught
      the first train.

Groß Ammensleben, Germany

Later, Mother would joke we'd marry millionaires
once we got to Canada, putting what was left

of her belongings into one small bag. Later, she'd say
        she tired of travelling, that in Canada,

she just wanted to stay in one place.   But that night,
she faced the wall
        and waved me away.

Sitting on the bed where Lida slept,
I watched faded floral curtains glide against dark glass,

                the world outside
          tilting to morning.

Checkpoint, British Zone, Helmstedt

The way I would tell it:

Through the night, three women flying
on bicycles. Mother hunched, sewing machine

strapped to her back, shoulders square and swaying.
       Lida, little bird,

fluttering between us, bent over homemade wine
to bribe the guards.   And me—

      (I could not read Mother's face.

      (I hadn't in years.
She was turned bone; nerve.

      (Our shadows skimming the road,
knees lifting skirts, wind shattering
the thin arms of trees, and all of us
following the length of river
      unspooling.

      (The pool of my grief
deep in me, undammed—

clunky old accordion
bouncing in my lap.   Father used to play.
      Peter used to sing. Hans,
           he'd tap the table in time.

Three women flying with what we could carry:

how I would tell it.

Tallgrass Psalmody

PART TWO

What called you home?

What waits wild
in the weeds
for you, hooded
& craning?
What crawls you
to the source?

                                        On my belly, I slide
                         one careful strand of grass from the earth.
            Gentle, gentle my father would coach *don't snap the root.*
I twist green in loops around my thumb, extract the pale thread
                                    seeking water, & speak—
                                        the stem breaks,
                                     connection severed.

                                    I touch tongue to root,
                         taste some lingering prayer,
                                      bite the soft end.

& what did you call home?

If it's sheer
indulgence for
flesh you
crave, warbling
in the woods,
quaking shapes
from soil—

                                                      seek
                                                     salvation
                                                     elsewhere.

                Flat in dry dirt, under rolling shroud of sky,

                                  I feel
                            for fieldnotes,

                      always unsure of what I am seeing:

wild geranium, lady's slipper, bunchgrass, bluestem, goldenrod,
                            clover cumulonimbus

Have you succumbed to despair?

Coo & caw,
vagrant, your sorry
burden lay bare.
There, a new
duet, a clutch
& clatter of bills
uplifting. If love
hooked you talon-first
from flight,
tangled you in
free fall, you'd too
submit to season,
hatch full-sung
hopes for
here, here, here.
High-bound,
hawks still
scratch out space
in narrow field,
rocky shore, park,
garage, suburb, skyscraper.

    When I close my eyes,

        the Black Raven comes clean across the field
        smashing nests half-built, abandoned.
        Cranes swing up condos, new bypasses bisect

            already invading
       brome, buckthorn, kentucky blue.

Will you show the soles of your feet?

Which death did you first heed?
The clearing, scraping, scrubbing?
The ploughing under? Prairie
fire prevention, aspen &
willow encroaching?
Or pollutants, powerlines,
pipelines seeping? How
many bright shells
did you crush,
thin, cool in
the bluestem?

                                    I make out the moon
                            mid-blink, afraid
                                        of what I still
                                          want.

vesper sparrow; lark sparrow; horned lark; bobolink; yellow rail; sandhill crane; northern flicker; upland sandpiper; short-eared owl

Will you study the span of your outstretched arms?

Watch yourself
wading out
to your puffed
chest, hovering
hands above
the swell &
know a river
welling will
bring everything
up, so recollect
each touch,
each hatched
plot, the taut
net expanding
far beyond your
reach.

What I still want:

one long, true story—good & true in the telling

to be absolved in the homecoming

these huddled birds as oracles,
each year returning in great guiding clouds or pillars
at night

to be undone & remade, like my body is not a memory
I keep confessing into some promise of land

Have you gone dormant?

An exodus
of self
may occur after all
your seeking
& this loss, too,
a resting
place.

                I'm sure—
                 I saw—

    in dreams, a dark house, an oak drowning, nests half-built,
              a riven plain.

             Unrelenting gale.

         Underneath, my Oma's voice—

How do you speak?

With conviction?
With wrath?
Turn from torpor.
Don't you know
fierce mystery
spins the undertow,
so rise from your
riverbed, slosh
in to shore—

                    as though
                    reborn,

                                      I slouch against a hollow.

Nearby, sparrows cluster in the brush,
                tremble their tails, dig in the dust.

> But how to hear anything
> beyond my own
> mouth?

A sparrow sings
bright at dawn.
She calls & listens
& calls
for response.

Un/Settling

1948 –

Aula Aunfong ess schwoa
All beginnings are hard

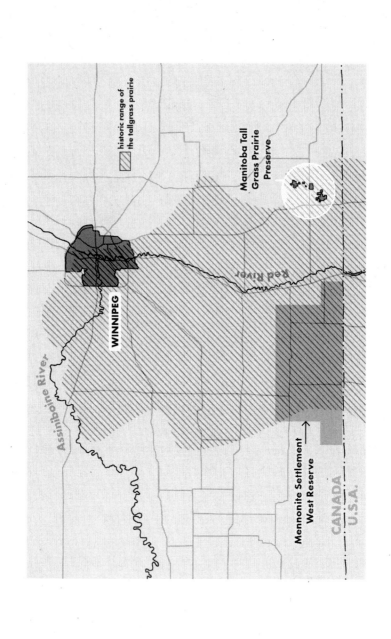

```
            the humble
    hands   of Christ       prepare
    the table
                    knead
                      hold
            flood                 fields
                    from
                    the pulpit
```

the story goes Anni sat herself on the corner of his
dark, heavy desk, watched him grade papers in fine red pen

the story goes she plucked a piece of candy
from a small glass bowl, twirled a hard,
sweet circle from plastic crinkling

the story goes she learned to know
Gerhard, the stern, shy schoolteacher-preacher,
the village's most eligible bachelor

born eldest son of Gerhard
G. H. Ens, born then moved in 1923
along with 20,000 other Russlaender Mennonites
to further settle Canadian prairie

the Canadian Mennonite Board of Colonization
immigrant-founded—by an earlier wave
of fleeing, farming Mennonites—
to coordinate this coming of Christ
followers, to tell the
martyred
legacy:

war
revolution
war
hunger
exile
        an inheritance   of turning
        to earth
                resisting the world
                learning
to
lean
        your
        body
                from
                        flesh
                through ice
to
carry
                your enemy
        safe to
shore
this
shore
of rich soil   shored up and
        tilled under
a promised   windblown   emptied
land   to cultivate
        with conviction
                      though enemies
        everywhere
so safeguard   the spirit
        and forgo
                despair—

```
the sparrow—
                there
                         see and know
the      LORD    watching
cover
                your
        hair


        (she misses dancing

        (she misses almost nothing
but the dancing


in thawing
        dirt:

                        a crocus
                and a child
        on her hands and knees
shrieks  full
        to the earth:

*purple!*
                in just a few hot months
                the beets
                will need
digging    the beans
           will need
                picking      the church
```

······················aching
······················and
······················sweating
it's either
quiet
or·······not at all
·········quiet
······················headfirst
················like a nuthatch
·········follow
the flash pattern
·········of the field
watch the conscience
················of a practical people·········a people
················persecuted
·········set·······apart/
······················saved
················reborn safe
in parcelled prairie·········prairie
·········set·······apart/
······················stolen
·········for····settler hands
······················driving ploughshares
······················deep
······················into
······················ancestral grounds

the teachings of Christ:

do not
adorn
your flesh
do not
take up
arms
do not
swear
an oath
avoid
the country
fair their
tractor shows
no card
games or
drink or
smoke or
sex so
      cling
           to the anguish
     of the faith
     stories   remember
         with holy
     severity

This is God's Own Truth / This is a crowbar

this is
your salvation

that first winter, Lida stayed in the village,
spoke German with relatives,
while Anni and her mother went to Winnipeg
to work and take English night school

Anni's high school scholarship, of course, meant nothing
here, so they cleaned wealthy women's houses
and with Anni's first pay,
she bought a fur coat—fox—red-brown

      (she brushes it like she would a cat,
brings it up against her cheek

slim-
winged and graceful   the tree
                          bank   and
              barn
                         swallow   streamline
      for trilled
                         flight

                          Look at the birds of the air ...
                Are you not much more valuable than they?

    the cliff
                        and northern
        rough-winged
    swallow

```
                dusky
                and dark in
        wide sky—coo-oo
                        waning song
of the   mourning
         dove     its pointed
                  tail and   dive   all
         mourn and
                        wallow


                   we mourn / here but we never know what for


                   not one lost
            from the flock
            they feed each other
                      read                 the names
of the never-home
                        a mirror
          of generations—
                   but each
             wave
sweeps          new
          shame   new
          calls for ex     communication
                   ev      angelism and
             with no       centre
                   no      place
sanctuaries
                           split
             open
             shut          out
```

(looking up from the garden,
her back between green beans, she can call a heaven
into being

tell again the old story of *Nachfolge*,
of Christ-following, sacrificing,
peacemaking, never resisting

      the tilling   of swords
                            to ploughs
   all up-   rooted

the story goes Anni bought her mother a house in the city
after she became engaged to Gerhard at Christmas,
shrouded by a sweet hush of snow

Anna was, at this time, reliant on her daughters,
since without a husband's death
papers, a refugee woman *could not remarry*
decreed the church council

      (she does not know her husband
dead, only knows herself
destitute

Anna lived there in her own home for twenty-five years,
and to her own home came Hans's letters

*Mama, are you healthy? Mama, I live not far from our old home.
Mama, I am somewhat worn out. Mama, I can hardly believe that
you are all still living ...*

observe at
           harvest
    a swarm of roots
    snarled
    white thread   knotting
          deep   soil   follow
    thin cords
to surface   where they cluster
at the kitchen table   of the family
                   farm
    the whole
         heart
                             or recall
                      the crane
              sweeping sky
        ochre
  with   flight   look   how they stand
  at the   shore
       unison-calling
       and each
            migration
   roosting together
to   survive

so Anni and Gerhard married and moved
to another small Mennonite village and here
their five children were raised

and a
                       good wife
managed
        the children
        gardens
        cooking
        pickling
        preserving
        cleaning
        mending
she managed and
                       maintained and

then the Red Cross letter came:

Anni's father died in 1942, though
records from the prison show
he never arrived

this story twenty years late
in widowing Anni's mother

*My dear Mama, my sister Anni says you are not entirely well. My
dear Mama, what hurts you?*

      (she creeps under covers, feels retreat
in her heart's rapid wings

      (Anni presses two fingers to her mother's wrist,
tracks her pulse as she calls for her children

                               home unwinds from the mouth

in the prairie church sanctuary:

                  a woman repenting her life
      during the war   her lack
                        of spiritual
diligence her   illegitimate
mewling
          children   her   children born of soldiers
her defilement   her
        submission   her
                    shame

                  If she resisted [the soldiers], she would lose
                                  the last two children

in the sanctuary:

                  silence

in the sanctuary:

                they made
                the women
                      repent

in the sanctuary:

                      Woman, come here!

in the sanctuary, the story goes:

De Manna oabeide enn de Frües hiele
        men work and women weep

        rocking
        the baby
              to sleep

    (she sings always
the same psalm in the little nursery
above the kitchen

    (and she does not speak about it,
not even to her husband

       the story goes Anni's eldest son watches
       the chair lean into and out of lamplight,
       bundled blankets squirming

       he watches the press of his mother's hand
       to the fine bone of her cheek

       and he learns to hate this hymn
       for making his mother cry, but then,
       the story goes, he sees The Blue Boy,
       feathered cap and curly hair
       cross-stitched and framed above the crib

    (the blue boy
she always grieves

Mama, why don't my sisters write to me? Have Anni and Lydia forgotten about me? My dear Mama, I would like to join my brother Peter ...

on the
shed   roof:

         a girl
sticks her
     legs   into bare
                     sun
        reads
             out   loud
    A Bird in the House

    while all around a
    momentous   migration
               unfolds

            flat on his belly, Anni's youngest tells stories
            to the kitchen heating vent, the place
            his imaginary friend hides, explains
            the screeching comes from Werner's new
            violin, much worse than the banjo, that Helen
            is singing Brahms, that Gear's come home
            bloody with fight, a Thiessen, of course,
            cheating at ball, and Annie,
            she's still reading up on the roof

            (in the house's warm exhale,
        he winds embroidery thread in circles,
        practises a fist

My dear Mama, if you can send me money, I need a lot of money.
My dear Mama, you would not recognize me …

Hans's story goes:

he lived with a Russian woman,
not his wife, and he would not part with her,
not even to come over

though the story also goes that sometimes
she begged him to leave

in her letters she wrote:

I often have nightmares.
Please forgive me everything.
I want nothing from him.

    (in a small black notebook, Anni writes:

we scarcely heard of the atrocities committed
against native Ukrainians or Jews

    (she writes:

all we knew, the Germans permitted us
to open our churches once more

    (she writes:

Mennonite young people
who worked as interpreters for the German occupation
were, by and large, treated well

    in stories, Gerhard always at his desk—
    he wets with his tongue one broad fingertip
    to turn the gospel pages while kitten heels
    click cracked linoleum from stove to sink

    (she pauses, crouches,
her youngest curled in the corner

   (she touches his soft hair,
plucks out the strand of yellow thread

   at night migrants
call out mid-flight   an echo seeking
     stars mapping
   magnetic
   fields   listening for water
          running
     even miles away

   (she often has nightmares

out of flight range
  and winging
  parallel along
  fragmented
     prairie lines
the migrants
  disorient in silent sky
      suburban
            city sprawl

the story goes it was a real movement,
those young people, and the world,
in the end, not so bad

stories of after-church scuffles, bush parties,
rock bands, ice skating, feminist fiction

and the family farm—well, what could be done?—
fertilized, specialized, mechanized, industrialized,
and eventually sold off

Mama, the Visa from the Red Cross helps nothing. Mama, you write that everyone is trying to help me, but it appears that it is all for nothing ...

a grebe   pulls
thick plumage tight to herself
      sinks
          low:

                 they'll

                               pluck out
          their own
          feathers
to feed
their young
                waiting   in furtive
          floating   nests

She took for him an ark of bulrushes ...
and put the child therein; and she laid it
in the flags by the river's brink

and the girl
on the roof
      looks up
           from
           the page
                      to see the whole earth
                      spilled from Your Hands
              and the
              geese
              grebes
              hawks
              swallows
              pipers
          cranes
          finches
          warblers
          and waxwings
      in rivers
moving north

Dear Mother Anna, I write you today with a heavy heart. Your dear Hans has died. He was beautifully dressed in a nice suit, the one you sent him, Anna. He was buried as they sang ...

the story goes Anni, Lydia, and Anna
made *zwieback*, served soup and pickles and cheese

        (she kneels alone in the dark
and remembers

I went to the kolkhoz and they made a coffin for me. I went to get him, but they would only give him to me on the third day ...

        (sometimes she lets herself forget

              Come, and let us return unto the LORD;
              for he hath torn, and he will heal us ...
              After two days will he revive us:

              in the third day he will raise us up

I am a foreigner here as he was. We are looking forward to a reply from you, as the nightingale looks for the summer ...

nightingales known
for their lament—they kill   themselves
        when caught
               in cages
               in endless   impossible
                       efforts   to go
    home

          What do you want to know about Mennonites? /
          do you understand we've come from memories?

probe   the prairie
               as a
               piper
        picking
soil   scraping
         nests   in dense grass
   rattling
song
         over fields   or come
             to this
             riverbank
        warbling
               answering   something

the story
from Hans's last letter

Mama, you walked with me from the edge of the village and gave me a homemade cloth for luck. On this cloth was the road to blossom, and meadow, and nightingales. I will take the cloth you gave me and will spread the cloth on the rustling grass under the rustling oaks ...

at the river's brink:

    kneeling

Mama, I will take the cloth you gave me and will spread the cloth on the rustling grass under the rustling oaks and all I have known will come to life on this cloth ...

at the river's brink:

                                  she puts her hands
                    in the current
                                  and holds
     looks
             listens
        tries
to learn a thing or two
about where
         she is spreading these   cloths
in the cold river   in the
rustling grass   under the reaching
       tree   this place
                    where

Tallgrass Psalmody

PART THREE

What story are you telling? Whose?

> *I will try to tell the truth*
> I say, crouching to pluck
> the broken blood
> feather from its slimy net of reeds.

Look how skin like wax
sheaths the hollow quill—

lift your head
& look.

Will you join the chorus?

An ongoing trill
follows the fringe
of bur oak & black
ash, stirs up
the overcast. O
downtrodden
stray, scrambling
for purchase
on a soft ridge
of song: this journey
winds through you
as guide.

                Once, I held out my hand
           & a nuthatch picked a peanut from
                   my palm, its feet both sharp & light,
                 its body fleeting & full & I think,
                            if nothing else,
     I can hold myself still enough to brush,
            even briefly,
               against this presence, airborne
                   & tipping
                 my whole face
                         to the rain.

After many minutes listening:

savannah sparrow; clay-coloured sparrow; red-winged blackbird; brown-headed cowbird; western meadowlark; mourning dove

Birds, like poems, follow the river.

Will you look well, dwell with, attend?

Above aspen &
maple, sage &
aster, you may
glean a landscape
inherited. Approach
unknowing
& singing praise.

                    In my Oma's margins: *How do you remember home?*

Have you recalled your flock?

The horizon shimmers oil
rainbows & weather
worsens. Gauge
the groundwater
you've sent away
industriously.
Measure
the severity
of the next
prolonged
drought.

Now, make
a racket.

One-third of migratory grassland birds
are nearing extinction
I read,
read again,
write
down.

A crow watching
from the hydro pole along the highway
tilts its head, extends its throat.

How did you come to this?

Every attempt
to return, trace
tributaries to
some source,
becomes another
rough meeting
of self. So return again,
restless with loss,
desire, never
hollowed or
whole. Here
is still something
of home.

                        Bending, I smear blood from my legs
                            cut by grass hip-high,
                      muggy buzzing at my ears,
                                intimate & ancient & latching
                                    sharp tongues to my skin.

& how will you go from here?

    This place where:

    spreading   these   cloths
    in the cold river, in the
    rustling grass, under the reaching
        tree—

                                I take note.

Oma Niebuhr/Anna (top) and Oma/Anni (right) serve a birthday party in Gretna, Manitoba, 1958.

NOTES

My Oma's story of migration and resettlement inspired the writing of this book. Though grounded in her true experiences and my memories of her voice, the poem is a creative re-imagining rather than a work of non-fiction.

Similarly, while *Flyway* is rooted in a local and specific tallgrass ecosystem, it is a work of artistic attention and not meant as a scientific resource. Those curious to learn more about the tallgrass prairie may wish to visit and support the Living Prairie Museum, a thirteen-hectare tallgrass prairie preserve and interpretive centre in Winnipeg, or the Manitoba Tall Grass Prairie Preserve, twenty square kilometres of tallgrass prairie located in southeastern Manitoba.

I quote from several poems throughout the book. These quotations are used gratefully with permission of the authors and publishers.

From "Prelude":

"thrones, / dominions of grass" is from "In the Hills, Watching," the first poem in Tim Lilburn's book *Moosewood Sandhills* (Xylem Books, ISBN 9781999971878).

From "Un/Settling":

"This is God's Own Truth" and "This is a crowbar" are from Robert Kroetsch's *Seed Catalogue* (Turnstone Press, 1979).

"we mourn / here but we never know what for" is from Don McKay's *Long Sault* (Applegarth Follies, 1975).

"home unwinds from the mouth" is from the section "Swarm" found in Jennifer Still's *Comma* (Book*hug, 2017).

"What do you want to know about Mennonites?" and "do you understand we've come from memories?" are from Patrick Friesen's *The Shunning* (Turnstone Press, 1980).

I also quote from the Bible, both the King James Version and the New International Version, in "Un/Settling": Matthew 6:26, Exodus 2:3, and Hosea 6:1-2.

The Low German phrases *"Aula Aunfong ess schwoa"* and *"De Manna oabeide enn de Frües hiele"* were sourced from *The Mennonite Low German Dictionary: Revised Edition* by Jack Thiessen (2018).

In "Flight," I quote from the "Village Report for Kronsthal, Chortitza Colony, Russia, 1942," in which the village mayor, district commissioner, and minister for the occupied territory write: "Now we are free! The brave German troops rescued us from the damn Bolshevistic yoke," following the German occupation of Kronsthal. This report was translated by Dora Epp and Anna G. Rempel and transcribed by Judith Rempel. It is available through the Manitoba Mennonite Historical Society.

T. D. Regehr's *Mennonites in Canada: 1939-1970: A People Transformed* (University of Toronto Press, 1996), was instrumental to the writing of "Un/Settling."

The anonymous quote "If she resisted, she would lose the last two children" was sourced from Marlene Epp's article "The Memory of Violence: Soviet and East European Mennonite Refugees and Rape in the Second World War" (*Journal of Women's History*, vol. 9, no. 1, 1997). Epp's article also included the quote "Woman, come here!" from Johanna Dueck's account of the war.

An estimated 10,000 Mennonite men were arrested and executed during Stalin's purges in the 1930s. The NKVD's black trucks would arrive in the middle of the night to take fathers, husbands, brothers, and sons away. These trucks were known as "black ravens" and are referenced throughout *Flyway*.

Mennonites immigrated to the Canadian Prairies in three major waves: the Kanadier from 1874-1880, the Russlaender from 1923-1930, and postwar refugees in the late 1940s. The Canadian Mennonite Board of Colonization, founded by Kanadier

Mennonites, assisted in the emigration of the subsequent two waves.

"A Brief History of the Johann Niebuhr and Anna nee Krahn Family"—as narrated by my Oma, Anni Ens—provided the lines Anni writes in a small black notebook on page 87.

Hans Niebuhr's letters to his mother, Anna Niebuhr, are excerpted throughout "Un/Settling," as are letters written by Vera, the woman who lived with Hans in Ukraine. The letter on page 45 was also written by Hans. These letters were translated and compiled by my uncle, Gerhard Ens, whose work of gathering and distributing our family's archives made this project possible.

Matthew Peters designed the maps on pages 20 and 72.

ACKNOWLEDGEMENTS

I wrote this poem while living in cities across the prairies, in lands marked by settlement made possible through Treaties 1 and 6, which disrupted the lifeways of First Nations and the Métis, who shared their knowledge of the land with newcomers. I am profoundly grateful to live and write in these prairie places.

Immense thanks to my editor Alice Major for following this poem along its many routes and helping it to land. Gratitude to Sheri Benning, Jeanette Lynes, and Laurie D. Graham for your deep insight and mentorship throughout the making of this project, and to Jennifer Still and Sandra Ridley for sharing seeds and suggestions.

Thank you to Turnstone Press for your passion and commitment and for bringing this book into the world. Thanks especially to Melissa Morrow for your careful reading and creative collaboration.

Thank you to Hans Werner for offering your Mennonite history expertise, and to my uncle Gerhard Ens for preserving our family's stories. Thank you to Norm Gregoire, community liaison for species at risk in the RM of Stuartburn, and Chris Friesen, coordinator for the Manitoba Conservation Data Centre, for answering all my questions.

To my brilliant peers from the University of Saskatchewan, especially Susie Hammond and Kathryn Shalley: thank you for giving your time, care, and wisdom to this poem. To Tea Gerbeza, Nicole Haldoupis, and Carley Mascher-Mayson, dearest firehearts: thank you for your sustaining support. For building nests with me, thank you: Corianne Bracewell, Jaclyn Morken, Katie Reimer-Wiebe, Michelle MacDonald, and Michaela Pries-Klassen.

Many people read many different iterations of this poem and shaped its trajectory. Thanks especially to: Molly Schaefer and Jillian Reimer for conversations around the kitchen table; Rachel

Burlock for every encouraging postcard and emoji; Laura McAlduff for requesting updates; Jonathan Dyck for sharing good books and ideas; and Karla Froese for first suggesting this was something I could write.

Finally, deepest gratitude to my family—my parents, Janet Loewen Ens and Waldy Ens, my siblings, Gerald, Lisa, Lynette, and Matthew, my nephew Roger, and all my aunts, uncles, and cousins. Thank you for your love and for sharing your stories. To my grandparents, Abram Loewen, Sarah Loewen, Gerhard Ens, and Anni Ens: your convictions continue to guide my life. Thank you for teaching me about home.